Dedication

This book is dedicated to the memory of my beloved mother.
I will always love you and cherish every moment lived by your side.
Thank you for showing me how wonderful life can be, when lived
with love, creativity and mindfulness.

contents

foreword

How do I begin to write this foreword and honour lovely Ishtar and her beautiful book? Perhaps I should begin with how our own story began. We became friends through social media – we came across each other's worlds and soon afterwards we picked up our most treasured letter paper, our prettiest envelopes and our most cherished stamps to start up a real correspondence.

Ishtar's correspondence is always so beautifully and meticulously crafted: sending cards that are stunningly embellished, illustrated, stamped and decorated lovingly with hand-made stickers. It was wonderful to see that our creative worlds were so closely aligned and familiar to each other.

When we met for the first time in Paris, Ishtar told me how much she wanted to write a book to showcase her work. I saw straightaway how strong it would be, and I encouraged her to find a publisher to suit her. A few months later, her dream came true and I'm delighted that it has.

Ishtar's world is sweet, poetic and generous. The Japanese inspiration behind all her creations takes us on an emotional journey. How can anyone resist these super-pretty ideas?

Huge congratulations, Ishtar, on this gift you've granted us. Flicking through these lovely, joyous pages is both good for the soul and the best catalyst for creativity.

Thank you for inviting us into your inspiring world.

Adeline Klam
www.adelineklam.com

introduction

I have many early memories of being given stationery and stamps as gifts. The way they were presented, their cute designs and the endless uses you could put them to, captured my heart in an instant! My favourites were from the Japanese brand Sanrio. Little did I realise that I would end up dedicating part of my life and work to creating my own!

To me, carving stamps is more than a craft. It is a moment of relaxation and meditation, when I devote myself to the joy of creating something with my hands. This – and the fact that you can use them in hundreds of ways – is why I love them.

Anything can inspire you to carve a stamp, if you look around. My designs are a result of my love of nature, Japanese culture, Kokeshis, Sakura flowers, bunnies, cats and childhood… These are my favourite subjects to draw and carve. What inspires you?

Sometimes, simple designs like flowers, or even basic shapes like circles and diamonds, are very effective. It's always a good idea to have plenty of these to use in your stamping projects, as they are very versatile.

We live in a time when we are slowly finding pathways to help us embrace and reconnect with our uniqueness and creativity, realising there's nothing we can't create with our hands and finding immense satisfaction in doing so. I know from experience that being creative and embracing your creativity gives you a sense of fulfilment and makes you happier in life.

I truly hope that this book contributes to that.

Ishtar

using this book

The book is divided into two sections. In the first section, the basics, you will be introduced to the stamp carving techniques. These are easy to learn and will enable you to develop and enhance your skills as you grow in confidence.

In the second section you'll find three chapters with a wide range of carefully selected projects that will allow you to apply your new skills and go on to use the many stamp designs that are in the book – there are more than a hundred in total. These projects include stationery sets, brooches, cupcake toppers, notebooks, Kokeshi cards, thread holders and much more!

Although these projects are all very different, they have a common aim: to be beautiful, fun and useful.

At the back of the book there are some templates that can be traced, carved, cut out and used to decorate stationery. Please be aware that the stamp design templates are real size. Do bear this in mind when choosing the size of your carving block.

Have fun, and I hope you, too, fall in love with stamping!

toolkit

1. Glue stick
2. Fabric ink
3. Pens and pencils
4. Craft knife
5. Ruler
6. Bodkin awl
7. Bulldog clip
8. Carving block
9. Bakers Twine
10. Washi tape
11. Rubber
12. Shrinkable plastic
13. Blank tags
14. Patterned paper
15. Hole punch
16. Sticky labels
17. Waxed cotton thread
18. Bone folder
19. Carving tools
20. Stamping ink
21. Scissors

carving tools

The kind of tools we use to carve our stamps were initially used for carving linoleum. Most linoleum carving tools come in a set with a handle and a number of different-sized gouges. These are numbered from 1 to 5, with the finest being no.1 and the broadest no.5.

Personally, I only use two of the gouges: a small one (no.1), for defining the design and carving the details, and a larger one (no.2) for carving larger areas.

A note on safety

Gouges are sharp tools, so please be careful when using them. Always carve away from yourself, making sure your hands are not in the way of your tool.

making your stamps

Learning how to carve stamps
is quite easy – I've had students
aged from nine to 60 years old
at my workshops, carving their
first stamps. To begin with, using
the gouges (knives) can be a little
tricky. It takes practice to achieve
a smooth, firm trace, but it can be
done – trust me!

i always tell my students that the secret to carving perfect stamps is love and patience.

positive and negative

The first thing you need to learn is the difference between positive and negative; it is the combination of these two concepts that, when applied to your design, will create your stamp.

Positive

Positive carving is everything that is taken out of the carving block or rubber. These parts won't ink, so they won't show when you apply your stamp to a surface (see left).

Negative

Negative carving refers to all the parts of the rubber or carving block that are not carved, and therefore stay on the stamp. These are the areas to which ink is applied, so they will be visible when stamped (see left).

Depending on your design, you may want to use a stamp with more positive parts or one with a larger negative area – it's up to you. Bear in mind that a negative-carved stamp will have the most visual impact, as it will hold the most colour.

carving the details

When you start to carve a design, always begin by defining the details. I highly recommend that, when carving a small detail such as an eye or nose, you should start carving around it first (if carved in negative). The consequence of not working in this order is that there will be insufficient support around the area of the detail and it will therefore break.

carving circles

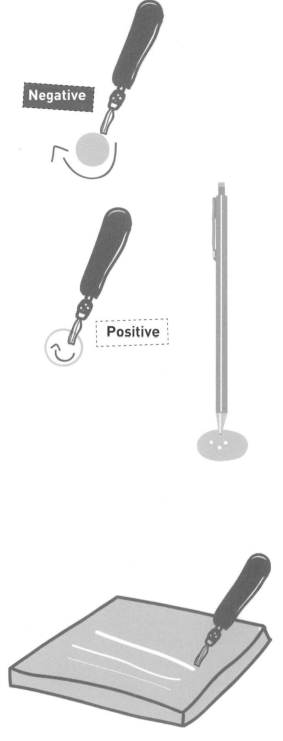

The trick to carving a perfect circle is to imagine your carving tool as a drawing compass. To create a negative circle, stick the tip of the gouge into the outside line of the circle you want to carve and, without moving it, slowly turn the carving block 360° to form a complete circle.

To make a positive circle the same process is applied, but instead of carving around the outside of the circle, carve around the inside.

To carve really tiny circles, use the tip of a mechanical pencil. Just press it into the carving block and lift. It will make lovely tiny dots!

creating lines

Making lines of the desired thickness doesn't depend only on selecting the right gouge, but also on applying the right level of pressure as you carve. The less pressure you use, the finer the carving line will be; the harder you press, the deeper the gouge will go into the block and the more you will carve out. With time, you will learn what level of pressure to apply to get the results you need.

When carving, keep your tool at a 30° angle, holding it like a pencil. This will help you to keep control of the tool and to obtain good results. Don't carve too deeply into the block; just far enough for your design to print when stamped.

If you've never made stamps before, first practise carving straight lines and curves on your carving block or rubber. Try to make your lines smooth and straight. This is the key to obtaining great carving results.

Once you feel confident with your lines, carve a simple stamp following the instructions on page 18, and move on gradually to more intricate ones.

let's make a stamp!

note

When transferring an image, bear in mind that it will be reversed.

1. Trace your design

Choose one of the stamp templates from pages 120–124. Place a sheet of tracing paper over your design and, using a no.2 pencil, trace the image. Place the tracing paper, pencil side down, on top of your carving block and rub with a coin or bone folder to transfer the image. Be careful not to move the paper, or the image may come out blurry. If you are doing a smaller design once you have traced it onto your block, cut around it with a craft knife. Then when you have finished carving, cut off any remaining bits of block you don't need; this also applies to a larger design. This way it will be much easier to carve and stamp.

2. Time to carve ...

Have you practised your lines and curves? Good! Start by lightly defining the outline of your stamp with a fine gouge, then, once you're happy with the shape, press more deeply. If your design has small details, carve around them first with your smallest gouge. Then, switch to a bigger gouge (no.2 to no.5) and carve the rest.

tip

When you want to change direction, rotate the carving block rather than the tool.

3. Ink, stamp and correct

The only way to know if the stamp is finished is by stamping it on paper. So, apply some ink, stamp it and carve away any parts that you don't want to be there.

stamping tips

1. Be sure to saturate your stamp with enough ink to cover the whole surface.

2. Press the stamp steadily and firmly onto your printing surface, taking care not to move it. Use the tips of your fingers if it's a small stamp and the palm of your hand for a larger one.

3. Leave the stamp in place for 5 to 10 seconds, to allow the ink to penetrate the paper or fabric, then lift gently to avoid smudging your freshly stamped image.

4. Allow the ink to dry for 1 to 2 minutes before touching.

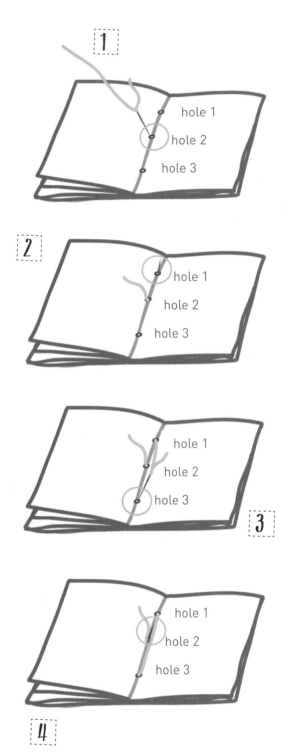

ledger binding technique

1. Starting on the inside of the spine, sew through hole 1. Leave 5 cm (2 in) of thread on the inside (this will be used at the end, to make a knot).

2. From the outside of the spine, sew back through hole 1.

3. Sew through hole 3, back to the outside of the spine.

4. Pass the needle through hole 2 again. The thread should now be on the inside of the book.

5. Tie the two ends together securely with a knot over the top of the long strand to hold it down and trim any excess thread.

paper spheres technique

1. Trace any of the sphere templates on page 118 you wish to use and cut them out. Using your cut-outs, make 10 circles in the same size of the desired sizes from your wrapping paper.

2. Fold each circle in half, with the right side of the paper facing inwards.

3. Open out one of the circles with the printed side facing down, then glue one of the folded circles on top, as shown. Repeat with the remaining folded circles, alternating the sides. You should end up with a neat stack

4. Lay the string in the centre of the open stack, with a short piece sticking out at the bottom. The length needed at the top will depend on where you want to hang the sphere.

5. Glue the two sides of the stack together to form a ball. See page 75 about how to add your stamped characters to your paper spheres.

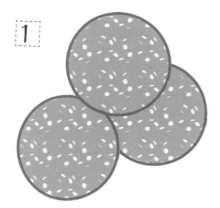

1

2

4

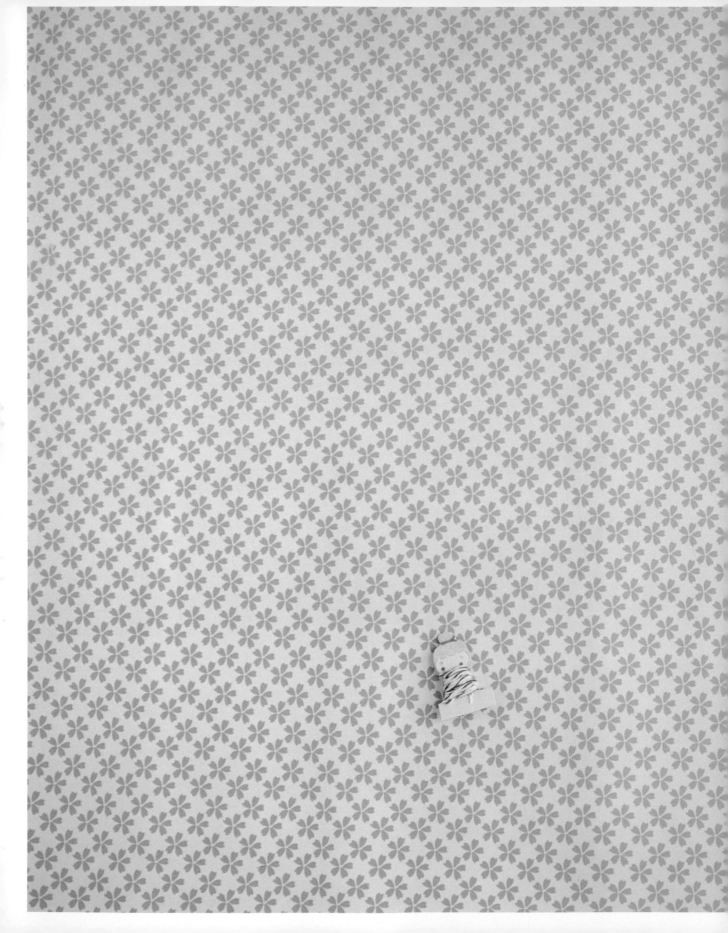

first projects

The following projects are designed to give you an introduction to the world of stamping. A simple stamp holds infinite possibilities for creation, decoration and embellishment.

place cards

There's nothing your guests will love more than finding these sweet little place cards on the table, when you invite them over to your next gathering.

materials

Stamp (see template on page 120)

Stamping ink

White card, cut into pieces measuring 6 cm x 4 cm (2¼ in x 1½ in)

1. Coat your chosen stamp, or stamps, with ink and use to decorate the card.

2. Let the ink dry before use.

Tip

Try embossing your place card with embossing powders and a heat gun to obtain a raised image. Embossing powders come in many different colours. Even gold and glitter!

cupcake toppers

This is an easy and fun way of jazzing up your bakes, simply by adding a decorative topper. Especially if it is one of a cute cat in a coat!

materials

Stamp for this project (see template on page 120)

Stamping ink

White card

Scissors

Toothpicks

Washi tape

1. Apply ink to your chosen stamps and press them onto the card.

2. Leave the ink to dry.

3. Cut out the images and stick a toothpick on to the back of each one using washi tape.

4. Add a fun touch with some washi tape folded in half, around the toothpick. Cut the end in a 'v' shape to make a flag.

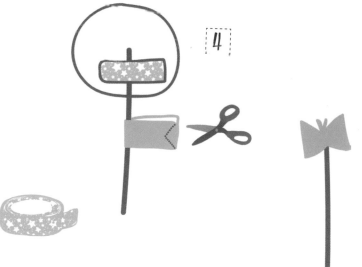

stickers

Everyone loves a pretty sticker and they are so quick to make. Create your own sticky labels to embellish your gifts, cards, notebooks and stationery.

materials

Stamps for this project (see template on page 120)

Stamping ink

Round sticky labels ranging from 1.5 cm to 4.5 cm (½ in to 1¾ in) in diameter

1. Apply ink to each stamp and press onto the sticky labels.

2. Leave the ink to dry then get sticking.

3. You can also add additional colour to your stickers by colouring them in with pencils, gel pens or felt tips.

Tip

Stamp on different types of sticky labels to change the look of your stickers: white, neon, craft, etc. And stick them anywhere and everywhere you possibly can: presents, notebooks, cards, and envelopes.

kokeshi thread holders

These dainty little thread holders are the perfect way to keep little samples of your favourite strings and threads to hand.

materials

Kokeshi stamps (see template on page 120)

Stamping ink

White cardstock

Scissors

Cotton thread

2. Cut out the figures, leaving a rectangular platform, 4 cm (1½ in) long and 1 cm (½ in) tall at the base.

3. Wind a different-colour cotton around each thread holder, creating a cute collection to gift or keep.

1. Apply some ink to your chosen stamps and carefully press them onto your card.

Tip

These little kokeshis are perfect for sending samples of your favourite threads and strings to your pen pals!

fabric card

This card is inspired by a Japanese folklore about the moon rabbit. The story is about a kind rabbit who saved a starving man, who in return drew the likeness of the rabbit in the moon for all to see.

materials

A sheet of white card measuring 24 cm x 15 cm (9½ in x 6 in)

White cotton fabric measuring 15 cm x 12 cm (6 in x 4¾ in)

PVC glue

Stamps for this project (see templates on page 120)

Fabric ink

Tip

Completely saturating the stamps with fabric ink will produce vibrant and rich colours. Press each stamp onto the fabric for at least 20 seconds, to allow the cotton to absorb as much ink as possible.

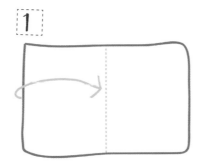

1. Fold the card in half, as shown above.

2. Glue the fabric onto the front of the card, carefully stretching it with the tips of your fingers to achieve a smooth result. Wait for it to dry.

3. Apply plenty of ink to your first stamp and press it onto the fabric, very carefully and firmly. Repeat with any other stamps you wish to add.

4. Once the ink of your stamps has dried, you can then use this card as a thank you note, get well card or even as something pretty to stick on your notebook.

koinobori thank you notes

I have always enjoyed Japanese celebrations. In May on Children's Day (Kodomo no Hi), families fly carp streamers to honour and wish their children a happy healthy life.

materials

White cardstock, cut into 8 pieces measuring 9 cm x 6.5 cm (3½ in x 2½ in)

Stamps for this project (see templates on page 121)

Stamping ink

1. Use pre-made cards or follow the instructions on page 31 to make your own.

2. Apply ink to your stamps, one at a time, and carefully print your design in the centre of each card.

Tip

Round off the corners of the cards using a corner punch machine.

plum-blossom garland

The Japanese have a deep appreciation of nature. Particularly during the spring when they celebrate the blossoming of ume (plum flower) and sakura (cherry flower).

materials

Stamps for this project (see templates on page 121)

Stamping ink

White cardstock

Scissors

Sewing machine

Thread

1. Ink and stamp your designs onto the card.

2. Leave the ink to dry, then cut out each shape.

3. Using a sewing machine, sew the shapes together one after the other, leaving a 1.5 cm (½ in) gap or no gap at all, in order to form a garland.

4. If you don't have a sewing machine you could attach the thread to the back of each shape using washi tape. Leave a length of thread at each end to attach to the wall.

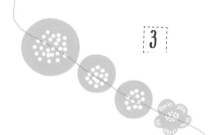

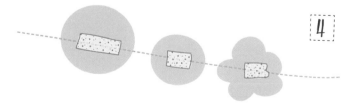

Tip

Try pairing the garland with others of different shapes and colours. Circles, scallops and stars work well together.

kokeshi card

I love kokeshi everything! Originally from the north of Japan, these traditional wooden dolls have become an icon all over the world.

materials

White card measuring 30 cm x 20 cm (12 in x 8 in)

Bone folder

Kokeshi stamps (see templates on page 121)

Multi-surface chalk ink

Scissors

1. Fold the card across the middle, creasing well with a bone folder.

2. Ink each stamp and print onto the card, assembling each part as shown below. Make sure the top of the head is at the very top of the card, where the fold is.

3. Once the ink is dry, cut into the shape of the kokeshi; be sure you don't cut out the top of head as this is where you need the fold to make your card.

memo pad

This is a nice way to make use of any discarded pieces of scrap paper, by turning them into a notepad. Stamp something cute on the cover and it will make you smile every time you write a note.

materials

Scrap paper

Scissors

Stamp for this project (see template on page 121)

Stamping ink

Bulldog clips

PVC glue

Paintbrush

(see template on page 121)

1. Cut out 100 pieces of scrap paper measuring 8 cm x 8 cm (3 in x 3 in).

2. Apply ink to the stamp and print the design onto each piece of paper. Allow to dry completely.

3. Stack the pieces neatly and hold them together by attaching bulldog clips to the left and right sides of the stack. (You could place pieces of card under the bulldog clips to ensure that there are no unwanted inky marks when they are removed.)

4. Brush the top edge of the stack with four to six coats of PVC glue, leaving the glue to dry between coats. Once the final coat is completely dry, the memo pad should hold together without the support of the bulldog clips.

Tip

This is the perfect project to make something both practical and beautiful. Write a sweet note for someone special and leave it somewhere for them to find.

brooches

brooches

I love shrinking plastic and how it offers so many
different possibilities. These brooches are just
the start; why not go on to make necklaces,
bracelets, rings and more.

materials

Stamps for this project
(see templates on
page 122)

Permanent black ink

White shrink plastic

Scissors

Oven

Baking tray

Wooden spatula

Super glue

Brooch pins

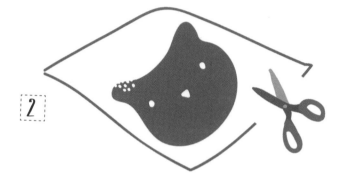

1. Coat each stamp with
permanent black ink and press
carefully onto the matt side of
the shrink plastic.

2. Leave the ink to dry, then cut
out your stamped images.

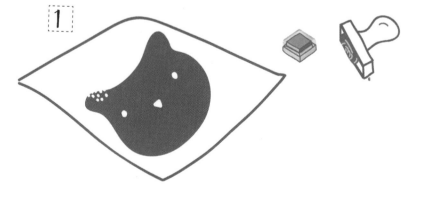

Note
The templates used for this
project already take into account
that the design will shrink. Bear
this in mind when creating your
own stamp designs.

3. Preheat the oven to 200°C (400°F/Gas Mark 6). Place the brooches on a baking tray and heat in the oven for 15-20 seconds or until the plastic has shrunk completely. It will twist and bend at first, before becoming flat again.

4. Remove from the oven and, using a wooden spatula, transfer the brooches onto a flat surface to cool.

5. Attach a brooch pin to the back of each brooch using super glue; hold the pin firmly in place until well adhered.

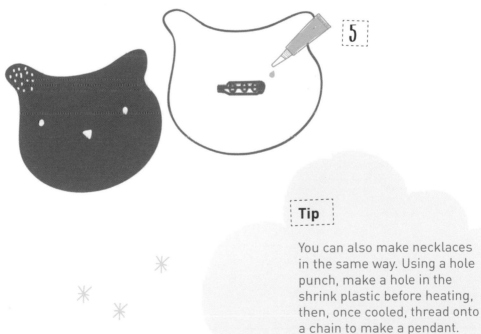

5

Tip

You can also make necklaces in the same way. Using a hole punch, make a hole in the shrink plastic before heating, then, once cooled, thread onto a chain to make a pendant.

stationery

Creating handmade stationery has recently experienced a revival. More and more people are reconnecting with the traditional methods of writing letters. What could be more fun and endearing than designing your own writing paper and using it to send a letter to a special friend?

stationery set

Writing and sending letters to friends is a passion of mine. I enjoy the process of preparing a little package, especially if it's made up of your own personalised, stamped stationery.

materials

Stamps for this project (see templates on page 122)

Multi-surface chalk ink in colours of your choice

White writing paper

White envelopes

1. Apply ink to your stamps and print the designs onto the writing paper and envelopes.

2. You could recreate the design shown here, or try out different colours and arrange the stamps in your own way.

Tip

Experiment with different types of paper – such as vellum or translucent paper – to create a variety of effects.

matchbook notepad

This is probably one the quickest and cutest notepads you can make. To use or to gift, fill it up with notes or observations, or even use it as a tiny sketching book.

materials

Matchbox notepad template (see page 118)

Tracing paper

Pencil

One sheet of cardstock

Scissors

Bone folder

Ten pieces of scrap paper measuring 6 cm x 5 cm (2¼ in x 2 in)

Stapler

Stamps for this project (see template on page 122)

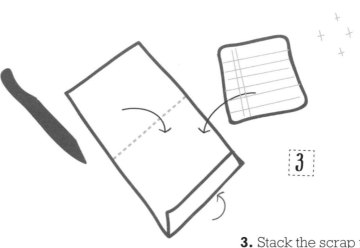

1. Trace the template using tracing paper and a pencil, then transfer to the cardstock and cut out.

2. With a bone folder, score along the dotted lines and fold the card to make the flaps.

3. Stack the scrap paper pieces neatly and place them inside the matchbook, underneath the small flap.

4. Staple the centre of the flap to hold the paper in place.

5. Decorate the outside of the matchbook with stamps.

Tip

You could also cover the matchbook with wrapping paper – glue the paper to the cardstock before cutting it out as in step 1 – or decorate it with washi tape.

usagui address labels

Rabbits (usagui) play an important role in Japanese folklore. These address labels will add a delightful touch to your letters and bring some character to your envelopes.

materials

Stamp for this project (see template on page 122)

Stamping ink

White card or paper

Scissors

1. Apply ink to your stamp and print onto the card or paper.

2. When it's dry, cut out your design.

3. When you have a letter or package to send, glue the label to the front and write the address of the recipient on it.

Tip

You can also use the labels as gift tags by simply hole punching one of your rabbit's ears, or even as little notelets.

house
envelope

house envelope

Celebrate a change of address or send a lovely letter to a friend with this adorable little house envelope.

materials

House template (see page 118)

Tracing paper

Pencil

Good quality or thick wrapping paper

Scissors

Bone folder

Glue stick (or double-sided tape)

Washi tape

Stamps for this project (see template on page 122)

Stamping ink

1

House number 1

1. Trace the template on the to reverse side of your wrapping paper and cut out.

2. Fold along the lines and crease with a bone folder.

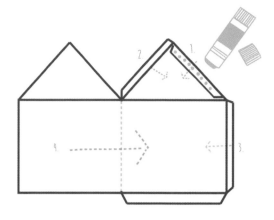

3. Glue the roof and side tabs and attach them to the other side of the house. Don't glue the bottom tab until you have slipped your letter inside.

4. Trace the front of the house onto another piece of wrapping paper and tuck it inside the house envelope. This will be visible from the outside. Stick an address label on the front as shown.

House number 2
1. Complete steps 1 to 3, as for the house one.

2. Cover the roof of the house with washi tape and trim off any pieces that stick out over the edge of the roof.

3. Cut several strips of washi tape and use them to make doors or windows or even to frame the house.

4. Cut a piece of washi tape 4 cm (1½ in) long, stick it on top of the roof and fold to make the chimney.

5. Apply ink to the postage stamp and mail bunny stamps and print onto white paper. Leave to dry, then cut them out and glue them onto the house.

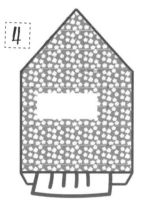

Tip

Have fun decorating your little house envelope, using your favourite papers, washi tapes, stickers and stamps. You could also draw a little cat waving from the window.

tea bag
envelopes

tea bag envelopes

If you are tea lover like me then you'll love these little teabag shaped notelets and handy envelopes. Great for writing notes to send to your friends.

materials

Teabag envelope template (see page 119)

Tracing paper

Pencil

Wrapping paper or scrap paper

Scissors

Bone folder

Glue stick (or double-sided tape)

Stamps for this project (see templates on page 123)

Stamping ink

Sealing wax stick or strong thread

White card

Washi tape (optional)

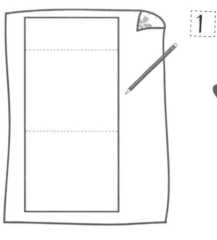

1. Trace the teabag envelope template using tracing paper and a pencil, then transfer to your choice of paper and cut out.

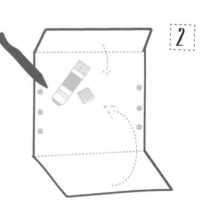

2. Using a bone folder, fold along the dotted lines and glue the sides of the envelope, as shown.

3. Apply ink to your stamps and use to decorate your envelope. (You may wish to print onto plain paper and stick this to the envelope, if made with patterned wrapping paper.)

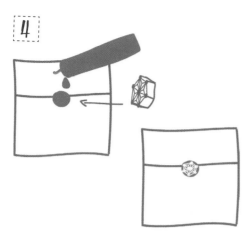

4. When you're ready to seal the envelope, you can do so using sealing wax and add your stamp to seal the envelope.

For the notes

To make a teapot notelet to put inside the envelope, print the teapot stamp onto white card and cut out. Alternatively, trace the template provided, cut out and cover one side with washi tape (see page 88 for detailed instructions). Trim off any untidy edges and write your message on the back.

kawaii party invitations

kawaii party invitations

A fun and creative way to make invites. Make them even more festive by sending them in an envelope with confetti or glitter, or even tiny pompoms!

materials

Stamp for this project (see template on page 123)

Stamping ink

White card

Scissors

Flower envelope template (see page 119)

Tracing paper

Pencil

Paper in any colour of your choice

Bone folder

Washi tape

Glue stick

1. Apply ink to your stamp and print onto the card. Leave to dry, then cut out.

2. Trace the template for the envelope using tracing paper and a pencil, transfer to paper of your chosen colour, then cut out.

3. Fold along the lines using a bone folder.

4. Tuck in the flaps and secure with a little washi tape.

5. Glue the stamp cut-out onto the envelope.

6. Decorate with bows, pink cheeks or a party hat made from washi tape.

Tip

To make each design a little different, you can vary the number of hair buns, by cutting off the one at the top or the two at the sides.

1

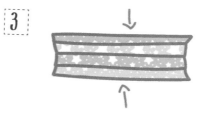

2

Washi tape bows

1. Cut a piece of washi tape 8 cm (3 in). in length.

2. Fold it in half, across the width, sticking the two sides of tape together.

 3

3. Mark the middle by folding it in half, lengthwise. Create the additional folds by continuing to fold your piece of washi tape in the style of an accordion, lengthwise

4. Press the folds together in the centre.

5. Cut a tiny strip of washi tape and wrap around in the middle of the bow.

4

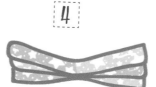

5

mini photo album

Here is one of my favourite ways to collect and keep little bits of paper and photos from my travels, by making a mini photo album. Make sure you stamp it and embellish with washi tape!

A piece of white cardstock measuring 47 cm x 10 cm (18½ in x 4 in)

Pencil

Ruler

Bone folder

Stamps for this project (see templates on page 123)

Scrap paper in assorted colours and patterns

Scissors

Glue stick

Washi tape

String or cord, 60 cm (24 in) long

1 round sticker

Double-sided tape

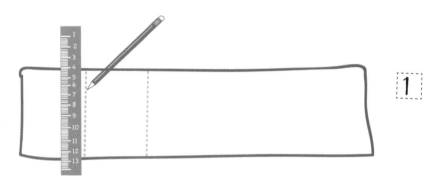

1

1. Using a pencil and ruler, divide the cardstock into seven panels, each measuring 6.7 cm (just under 1½ in) in width.

2. Using a bone folder, score along each line and fold the panels alternate ways, so you create a concertina effect.

3. Apply ink to your chosen stamps and decorate the panels that are on the outside when closed. Leave to dry.

2

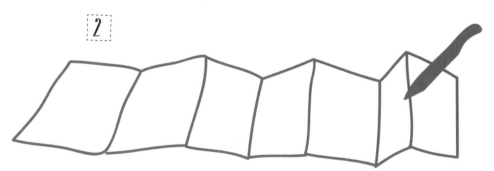

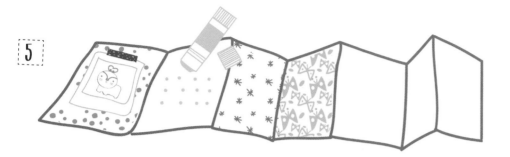

4. Select six pieces of scrap paper and cut into pieces exactly the same size as the card panels.

5. Glue one piece of scrap paper onto each panel that isn't stamped.

6. Stick a strip of washi tape along each fold.

7. Attach the string to the outside of the first panel using a round sticker. To hold the album closed, wrap the string around the outside.

8. Use double-sided tape to fasten your photos into the album. If you wish, you could mount the photos on plain backing paper and stamp the top with the washi tape stamp.

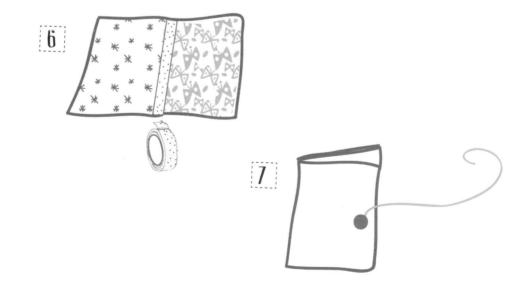

mini books

mini books

Mini things are, and will always be, adorable. These teeny tiny notebooks are perfect to fit in an envelope along with a letter you are sending to family or friends.

materials

1 piece of white cardstock measuring 8 cm x 5.5 cm (3¼ in x 2¼ in)

5 pieces of scrap paper, each measuring 7.5 cm x 5 cm (3 in x 2 in)

Bone folder

Paper clips

Pencil

Ruler

Awl

Waxed cotton

Sewing needle

Scissors

Stamps for this project (see template on page 123)

Stamping ink

1. Place the card with the reversed side facing up, then form the scrap paper into a neat pile and place it centred on top of the card.

2. Using a bone folder, fold the pile of card and paper in half lengthways.

3. Open up the pages and secure them with paper clips.

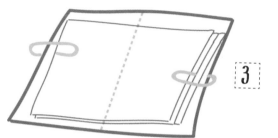

4. With a pencil, mark three points along the fold: the first two 1.25 cm (½ in) from the top and bottom edges, and the third exactly halfway between these two. Make a hole through the stack at each of these points, using an awl.

5. Bind the spine using the waxed cotton, following the ledger binding technique (see page 72).

6. Using your hands, press the book to flatten.

7. Apply ink to the stamp and decorate the cover of your mini book.

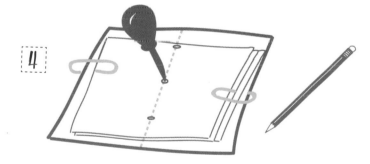

Tip

As an alternative to the stamp design, you could decorate the book with washi tape or cover it with pretty paper.

paper spheres

This is a quick and easy-to-make decoration that gives great results. They'll look beautiful anywhere and everywhere you hang them.

materials

Stamps for this project (see templates on page 123)

Stamping ink

White card

Scissors

Paper sphere templates (see page 118)

Tracing paper

Pencil

Wrapping paper

Glue

String or twine, 30 cm (12 in) long

1. Apply ink to your chosen stamps and print onto card.

2. Leave to dry, then cut out the designs. Your stamped design will need a back so make sure you stamp two of the same design or cut out a identical shape, from blank paper to match up with your front stamped design.

3. Make your paper sphere as per the instructions on page 21. Leave some extra string below or above your sphere, depending on where you would like to attach your stamped character.

4. To attach your stamped decoration to the string take your two pieces, front and back, glue and sandwich the thread in between. Hold in place until it is secure then leave to dry.

clutch notebook

I'm always on the lookout for beautiful notebooks but making your own is even more satisfying. These clutch notebooks are must-keep journals and they also make lovely gifts!

materials

Pencil

Ruler

1 sheet of watercolour paper, 120 gsm, measuring 30 cm x 15 cm (12 in x 6 in)

Bone folder

Glue stick

Wrapping paper measuring 30 cm x 15 cm (12 in x 6 in)

20 sheets of paper, measuring 20 cm x 14 cm (8 in x 5½ in)

4 bulldog clips

Awl

Sewing needle

Embroidery or book-binding thread (waxed cotton)

Scissors

Stamps for this project (see templates on page 123)

Stamping ink

1. Using a pencil and ruler, divide the watercolour paper into three panels, two measuring 12.5 cm (5 in) and the third 5 cm (2 in) (see below).

2. Using a bone folder, score and fold along the pencil lines.

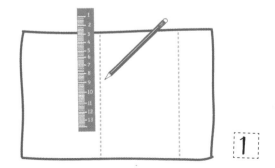

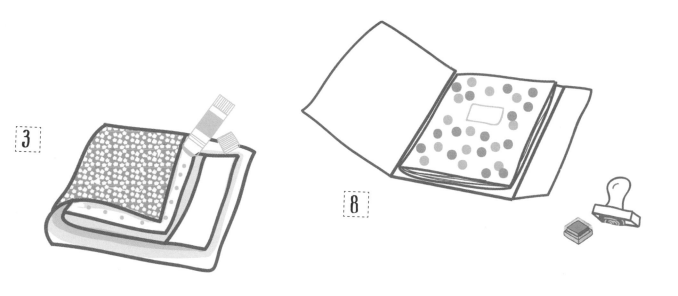

3. Glue the outside of the cover and attach your wrapping paper. Put the cover to one side.

4. Fold the 20 sheets of paper in half using a bone folder. These will make the pages of the book.

5. Stack the pages neatly and tuck inside the cover. Open out the book, inside pages facing up, and secure with bulldog clips.

6. With a pencil, mark three points along the spine: the first two at 4 cm (1½ in) from the top and bottom edges and the third one halfway between these two. Make a hole at each of these points, all the way through the book, using an awl.

7. Bind the spine using the needle and thread, following the ledger binding technique (see page 72) Press the book to flatten it out.

8. Apply ink to your chosen stamps and use to decorate the inside pages.

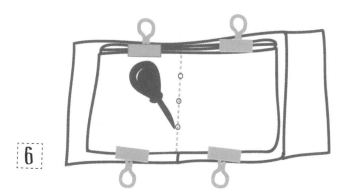

Tip

You can create clutch notebooks of any size by simply increasing the paper size and using the same technique.

stapled notebook

This is a very easy way to make your own personalised notebook. Simply combine different types of paper and stamp your way through it.

materials

10 sheets of A4 paper (to make a 20-page notebook)

1 sheet of white A4 card

Bone folder

Flower and animal stamps (see templates on page 123)

Stamping ink

Bulldog clips

Pencil

Ruler

Piece of string 17 cm (6¾ in) long

Long-reach stapler

Tiny craft bell

Craft knife

Fabric tape or washi tape

1. Fold the sheets of A4 paper in half and stack them neatly to form an A5 notebook.

2. Using a bone folder, score and fold the card down the middle. This will be the cover of the notebook.

3. Apply ink to your chosen stamps and use to decorate the cover.

4. Tuck the folded sheets of paper inside the cover, making sure the edges are lined up neatly. Crease the papers with the bone folder to help get them in neatly.

COVER

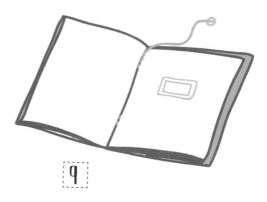

5. Unfold the notebook, cover facing upwards. Keep the pages in place using bulldog clips.

6. Use a pencil to make two marks along the fold, 5 cm (2 in) from the top and bottom edges.

7. Place the string along the underside of the fold, so that one end sits just below the top pencil mark and the other end sticks out of the top of the notebook.

8. Staple over the marks with the long-reach stapler, making sure the string is fastened on the inside of the notebook.

9. Attach the bell to the free end of the string.

10. Remove the clips and close the notebook. If you want a perfect finish, trim the edges using a ruler and craft knife.

11. For that finishing touch, attach fabric tape or washi tape along the spine.

Tip

Try alternating the pages with different coloured paper, or stamping the interior pages with any design of your choice.

accordion
folder

accordion folder

This is a pretty, practical folder that takes no time to make. Perfect for storing your postal stamp collection or paper ephemera.

materials

Pencil

Ruler

1 sheet of card in any colour of your choice, measuring 29 cm x 17.5 cm (11½ in x 7 in)

Bone folder

Wrapping paper measuring 29 cm x 17.5 cm (11½ in x 7 in)

Glue stick

5 envelopes, roughly 17 cm x 11 cm (6 in x 4 in) size

Scissors

Eyelet punch (such as Crop-a-dile)

2 eyelets

Short piece of thin elastic

Wooden button

PVA glue

Stamps for this project (see templates on page 124)

Stamping ink

White paper

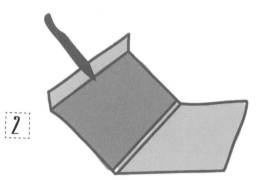

1. Using a pencil and ruler, along the width of the card draw a line at 3.6 cm (1⅜ in), 4.8 cm (1⅞ in), 16.3 cm (6⅜ in) and 17.4 cm (6⅞ in) from the top (see below).

2. Using a bone folder, score and fold along the lines.

3. Glue the outside of the card using the glue stick, and cover with your wrapping paper.

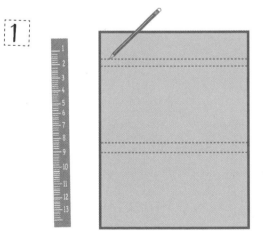

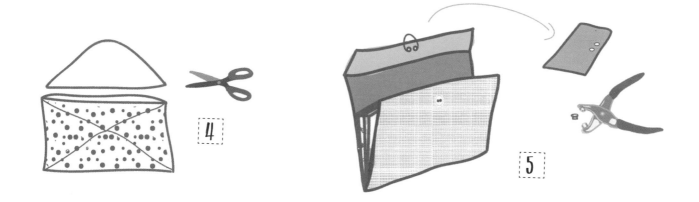

4. Cut the flap off each of the envelopes, then using the glue stick, glue the sides of the envelopes together and to the inside of the folder, as shown below.

5. Punch two holes in the centre of the upper flap and insert an eyelet into each one. Pass the elastic through the eyelets and make a knot on the inside, leaving a small loop on the outside.

6. Using PVA glue, stick the button onto the front flap, in line with the elastic loop.

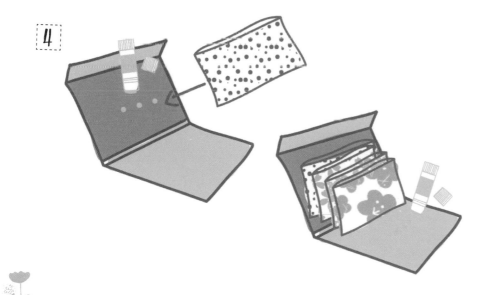

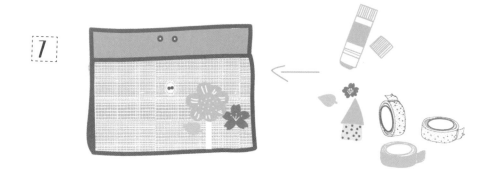

7. Apply ink to your stamps and print onto white paper. Leave to dry, then cut out and stick onto the folder. Alternatively you could decorate your folder with washi tape.

How to decorate your folder with washi tape motifs
1. Choose a stamp template from the selection included (see pages 120-125), then trace it onto vellum paper.

2. Turn the paper pencil side down and cover with washi tape.

3. Cut out the template and stick to the folder using a glue stick or double-sided tape.

4. Add any details using a white gel pen or permanent marker.

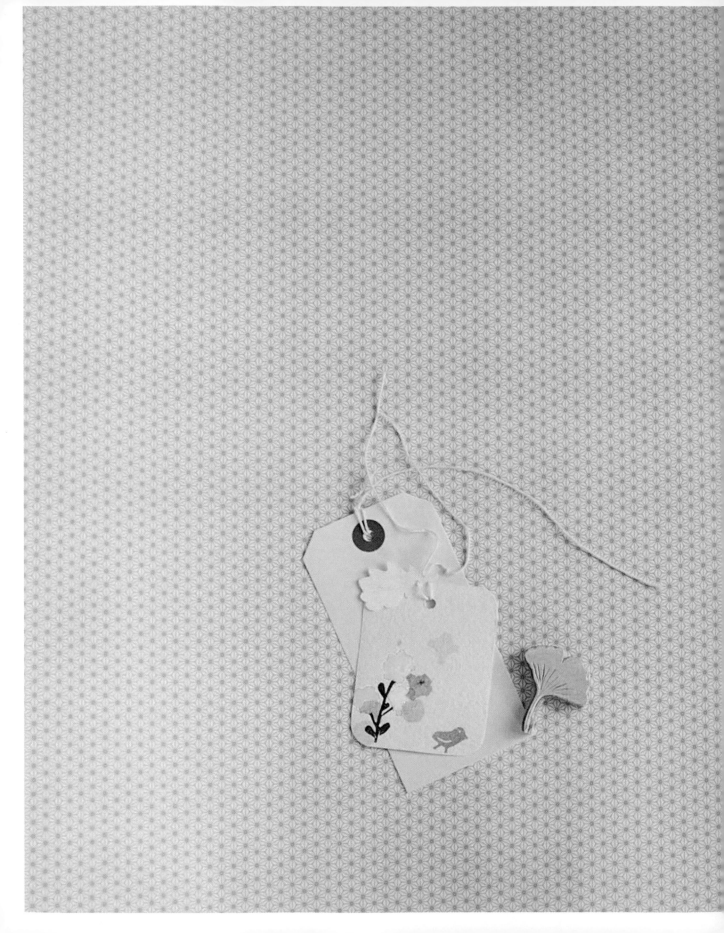

gift wrap

The Japanese put a lot of effort into gift wrapping. Paying special attention to the way you wrap a present not only adds aesthetic value, it also makes the gift more meaningful. The packaging should be almost as pretty as the gift inside! These ideas will help make your gifts stand out from the rest.

forest tags

Adding an adorable tag to a package is the best way to embellish any gift. These nature inspired tags are so cute, you will want to keep them all for yourself.

materials

Stamps for this project (see templates on page 124)

Multi-surface chalk inks (or any stamping ink)

Assortment of scrap paper and card

Scissors

Sticky foam pads

Hole punch

Different types of string or twine

1. Print your stamps onto paper or card using the inks of your choice. Leave to dry.

2. Cut the paper or card into the desired shapes and sizes for your tags. Alternatively, cut around the stamped designs and stick the shapes onto gift tags using sticky foam pads, to create a raised effect.

3. Punch a hole in each tag and attach string or twine.

Tips

Use different kinds of paper and other materials, like watercolor paper, cardstock, vellum, tracing paper or even wood. You could also cover the backs of your card tags with washi tape before cutting them out.

cat gift bags

These cat bags are perfect for party favors and they are so kawaii. Plus they only take a few minutes to make.

materials

Paper bag

Pencil

Scissors

Round sticky label

Stamps for this project (see templates on page 124)

Black stamping ink (use permanent ink if your paper bag has a glossy finish)

Washi tape

1. At the top of the paper bag draw the shape of the cat's ears (as shown above) and cut out.

2. Stick a round label in the centre of the bag and print on the eyes and a nose using your stamps.

3. Cut some thin strips of washi tape and use to make whiskers.

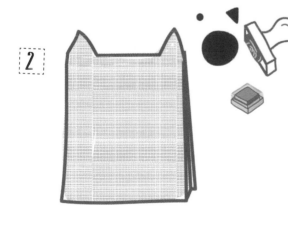

wrapping paper

Add a personal touch to your gifts by making your own wrapping paper. You can't get more special than that!

materials

Plain paper, large enough to cover your gift

Stamps for this project (see templates on page 124)

Stamping ink, in one or more colours

1. Lay out your paper to the size you require on a flat surface. Alternatively you can work on a whole roll, but stamp sections at a time to make it more manageable.

2. Apply ink to your stamps and print onto the paper in a repeated pattern or at random, (see below for ideas).

Straight

Alternate

Half Drop

Random

money
envelopes

money envelopes

It's a popular tradition in Japan to gift money depending on the occasion. This is a modern variation that can be used as a stationery envelopes as well.

materials

Money envelope template (see page 119)

Tracing paper

Pencil

Wrapping paper measuring 17 cm x 17 cm (7 in x 7 in)

Scissors

Bone folder

Stamp for this project (see template on page 124)

Stamping ink

Fabric measuring 17 x 17 cm (7 in x 7 in) (if doing the fabric option)

Piece of card measuring 17 cm x 17 cm (7 in x 7 in) (if doing the fabric option)

Glue stick or PVC glue (if doing the fabric option)

1. Trace the template using tracing paper and a pencil, then transfer to the reverse side of your wrapping paper.

2. Cut out the shape, then score and fold along the lines using a bone folder.

3. Glue the bottom and side flaps as shown (see right).

4. Decorate your envelope by stamping onto it or by sticking on your cut-out stamped designs onto it as with the Forest tags (see page 92).

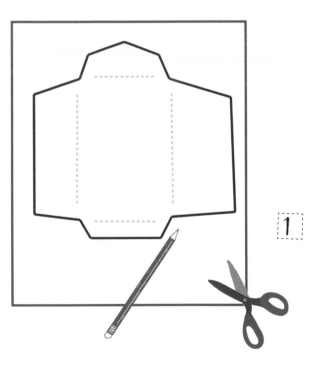

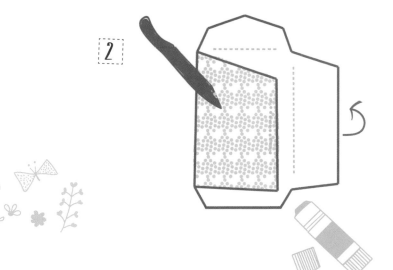

2

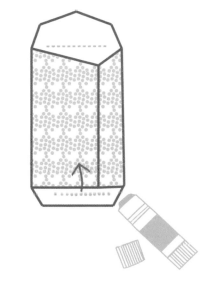

3

Fabric option

You can also make this
envelope with fabric by simply
gluing the fabric onto the card
using PVA glue. Then trace
your template onto the card
and cut out. Fold along the lines
as per the instructions for the
paper envelope.

4

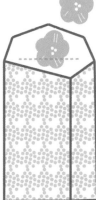

japanese
candy bags

japanese candy bags

Present your friends with some sweet treats packed in these colourful Japanese paper bags. You can also use them to wrap up smaller presents.

materials

Wrapping paper measuring 15 cm x 11.5 cm/6 in x 4½ in (for 1 bag)

Washi tape

Stapler (optional)

Card

Scissors

Stamps for this project (see templates on page 124)

Stamping ink

Hole punch

String or twine

1. Place the wrapping paper horizontally in front of you. Fold both sides into the centre and stick the edges together with a piece of washi tape, reaching from top to bottom.

2. Fold the bottom edge upwards and tape in place.

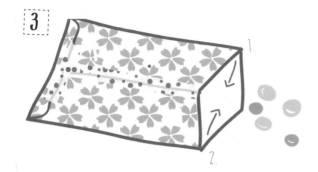

3. Open the bag at the top and flatten out so corners 1 and 2 meet.

4. Fill the bag with sweets and fold the top to close. Secure with washi tape or a staple.

5. Cut out a small round tag from a piece of card and decorate using one of the stamps.

6. Punch a hole in the tag, attach a piece of string or twine, then stick to the candy bag with washi tape.

Tip

Try making the candy bags with vellum or tracing paper. The result is just as beautiful and you can see some of the bag's contents from the outside.

matchbox wrapping kit

matchbox wrapping kit

Surprise your friends by making them this present pack. Include some tissue paper, tags, string, washi tape and one of your very own hand carved stamps.

materials

Matchbox template (see page 119)

Tracing paper

Pencil

Patterned cardstock (or wrapping paper glued onto plain cardstock)

Scissors

Bone folder

Ruler

Glue stick

Tissue paper

Stamp for this project (see template on page 125)

Little trinkets

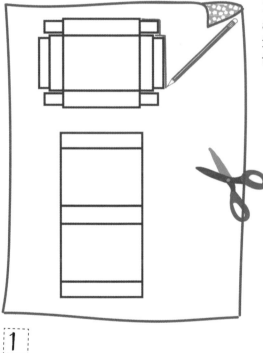

1

1. Using tracing paper and a pencil, trace the template for the matchbox base, then transfer to the cardstock.

Tip

You could make this project using recycled cardstock from pretty packaging.

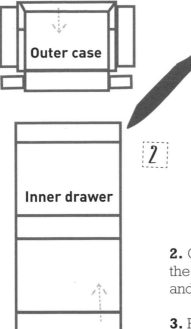

Outer case

Inner drawer

2

2. Cut out, then score along the lines with a bone folder and ruler.

3. Fold the flaps of the drawer and glue them in place as shown below.

4. Repeat steps 1 to 3 for the outer case.

5. Fill the drawer with trinkets such as hand-carved stamps, a little reel of twine, round stickers and mini tags and place inside the outer case.

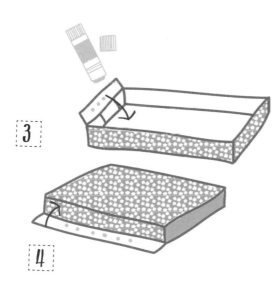

3

4

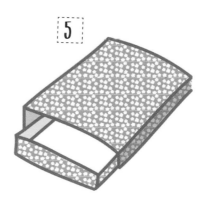

5

With
love
to
Paul
and
to
Philip

Copyright © 1995 by Ruth Heller
All rights reserved. This book, or parts thereof, may not be
reproduced in any form without permission in writing from the publisher.
A PaperStar Book, published in 1998 by The Putnam & Grosset Group,
200 Madison Avenue, New York, NY 10016. PaperStar is a registered
trademark of The Putnam Berkley Group, Inc. The PaperStar
logo is a trademark of The Putnam Berkley Group, Inc.
Originally published in 1995 by Grosset & Dunlap.
Published simultaneously in Canada. Printed in the United States of America.
Library of Congress Cataloging-in-Publication Data
Heller, Ruth, 1924-   Behind the mask : a book about prepositions /
written and illustrated by Ruth Heller.   p.   cm.
Summary: Explores through rhyming text the subject of prepositions and
how they're used.   1. English language—Prepositions—Juvenile literature.
[1. English language—Prepositions.] I. Title.
PE1335.H45   1995   428.2—dc20   95-9535   CIP   AC
ISBN 0-698-11698-4

1   3   5   7   9   10   8   6   4   2

RUTH HELLER

WORLD OF LANGUAGE

BEHIND THE MASK

A Book About Prepositions

Written and illustrated by
RUTH HELLER

The Putnam & Grosset Group

Of PREPOSITIONS have no fear.

They help to make directions clear.

beyond
this
green,
reptilian
beast . . .
past its hungry,
gaping
mouth . . .

veer directly . . .

to the south,
toward a place
where mermaids flock
upon,
beside,
and **near** a rock.

One
hundred
twenty
paces
west . . .
the
treasure
lies
inside
this
chest.

PREPOSITIONS
are the best!

They're never alone.
They're always
in phrases . . .   behind   the
                                                                masks
                                                                and . . .

through the mazes.

They almost always start the phrase . . .

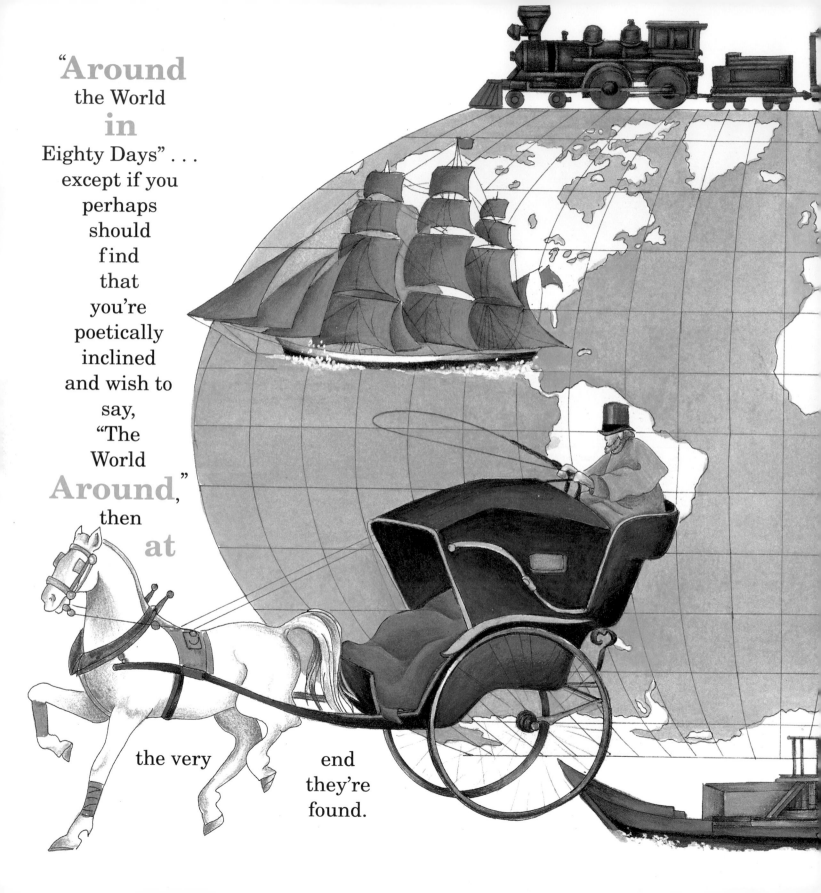

"**Around** the World **in** Eighty Days" . . . except if you perhaps should find that you're poetically inclined and wish to say, "The World **Around**," then **at** the very end they're found.

Of
PREPOSITIONS
have
no
fear.

In
phrases
only
they
appear.

So
if
a
word
upon
this
list
without
a
phrase
is
found . . .

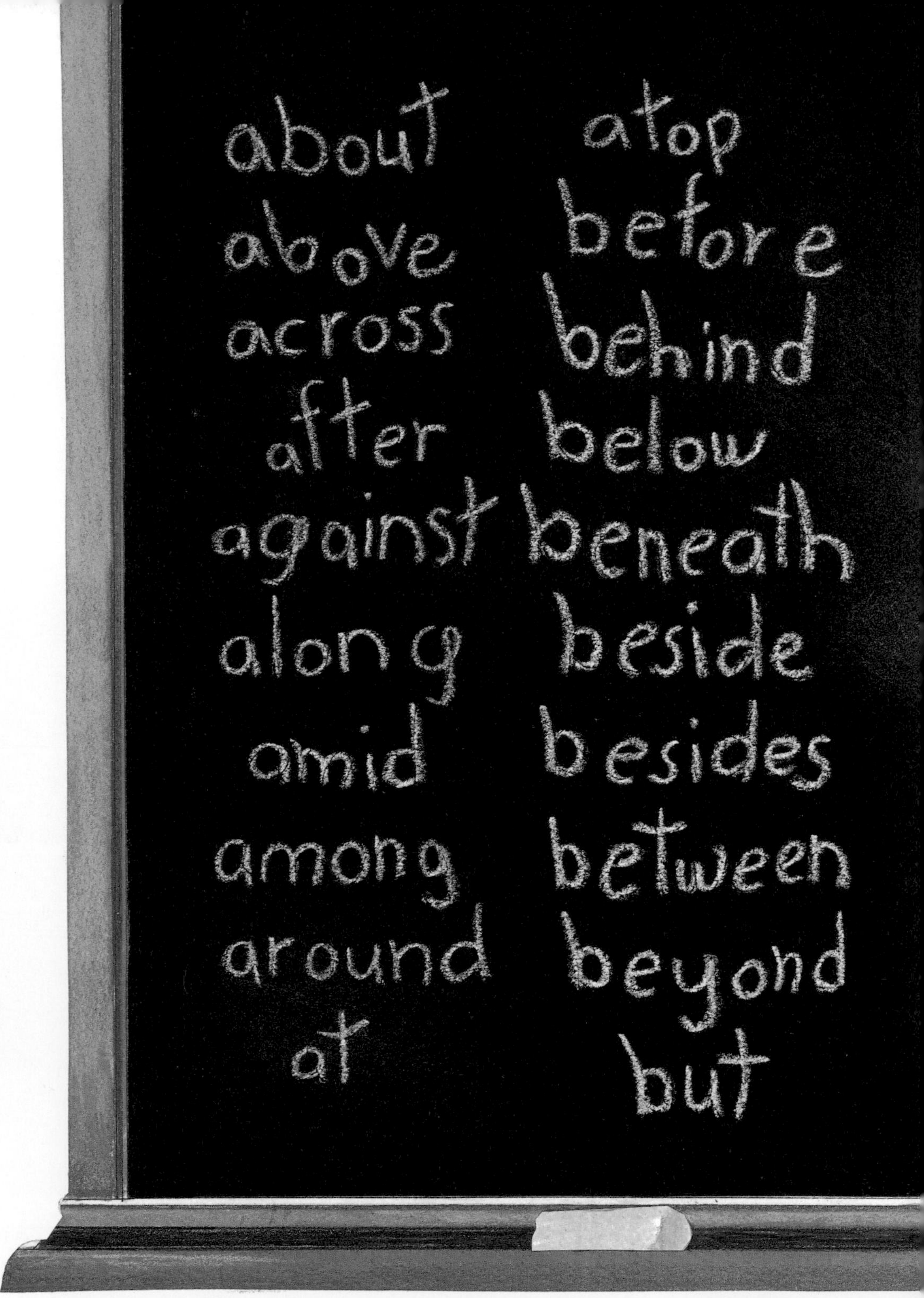

about   atop
above   before
across   behind
after   below
against   beneath
along   beside
amid   besides
among   between
around   beyond
at   but

by
concerning
down
during
except
for
from
in
inside
into
like

near
of
off
on
onto
out
outside
over
past
regarding
since

through
throughout
to toward
under
underneath
until
unto
up upon
with
within
without

as when I say . . .

"Please step inside,
come in,
and
look around."
It's not a
PREPOSITION,
so
take a careful look.
It's
probably an
ADVERB

and is **in**

another
book.

So you will never be confused . . . here are some rules
that can be used.
The cow jumped **over** the moon.

The
dish ran
away
with the spoon.
PREPOSITIONS tell you where.

They
tell you how . . .

and
when.
Please don't
wake us
until
ten.

Into
means
"to enter,"
and
that's the reason
why . . .
"Step **into** my parlor,"
said
the
spider
to the fly.

But if inside *already* is what you really mean . . .
then . . . eating bread and honey . . .

in
the parlor
is the queen.

Be angry **with** a person, but angry **at** a thing.
I'm angry **with** Jack
and
I'm angry **with** Jill . . .
but,
I'm angrier
still
at
the
pail
and
the
hill.

Between must be said when referring **to** two, and **among** when referring **to** more.

The ten is **between** the king and the queen . . .

and the five is **among** these four.

Say, " different **from**," not "different than."
Find the odd one if you can.

This is a test. . . . Which one is different **from** the rest?

One PREPOSITION is one too many **in** sentences that don't need any.

Where have you been at?

And two PREPOSITIONS aren't better than one. . . .
Icarus flew **near**,
not near to, the sun.

One is
enough . . .

to
tell
you
where.

They
fell
off,
but not
off of,

the red
rocking chair.

Despite what you have heard,

sometimes PREPOSITIONS can be more than

The deer is **in front of** the camel. . . .

The lion's **in back of** the horse.

just one
word.

These are
PHRASAL
PREPOSITIONS

and . . .

here are more
of them, **of** course.

on account of

according to   as of   owing to
apart from   because of   in spite of
by means of   instead of   in regard to
in addition to   next to   in view of
as far as   out of   in place of

PREPOSITIONS, **in** this modern day,
at the end **of**
a sentence
are sometimes okay.
So it isn't an error . . . it isn't a sin
to say,
"It's the room that I was playing
in."
But those who are graced
with
impeccable taste
will insist upon saying,
"It is the room **in** which I was playing."